SOUL STAR ~ CHILD OF THE UNIVERSE

SOUL STAR ~ CHILD OF THE UNIVERSE

SOUL POEMS AND HEART WISDOM

MADELINE K. ADAMS

ROSLYN PUBLISHING

The intent of the author is to offer information of a general nature to
help the reader in their quest for soul wellbeing.
The information given in this book should not be treated as a
substitute for professional medical advice and any use of information
is at the reader's discretion and risk. Neither the author nor the
publisher can be held responsible for any loss, claim or damage
arising out of the use, or misuse, of suggestions made, the failure to
take medical advice, or for any material on third party websites.

First Published December 2019. A catalogue record of this book is
held at the National Library of New Zealand.
ISBN: 978 0 473 50741 1(Kindle)
ISBN: 978 0 473 50739 8 (Softcover)

Roslyn Publishing Limited
P O Box 32276
Auckland, 0744
New Zealand

Cover Image: Alexander Andrews ~ *The Heavens*

An invitation to know the wisdom of your heart

CONTENTS

Introduction   ix

Part I
AWAKEN THE CREATRESS

A Creatress Speaks   3
1. Feminine Essence   5
   Psyche   7

Part II
THE INNER JOURNEY

2. Solitude   11
3. Cave Dweller   13
4. Soul Wisdom   15
   You Are Not Alone   17
5. Soul's Loving Guidance   19
6. Breathe is Life   21
7. The Inner Path   23

Part III
DEEPLY FEMININE MYSTERY

8. I am a Creatress   27
   Creatress   29
9. Secrets of a Creatress   31
   My Inner Child   33
10. Darkness and Mystery   35
11. La Vierge Noire   37
    Vierge Noire   39
    Pure Essence   41
12. Womb Magic   43
    Love Token   45
13. A Persephone Woman   47
    Persephone   49

14. Laws of the Underworld   51

Permission   53

The Ways of A Modern Mystic   55

15. Mystery and Magic   57

La Vierge Enciente   59

A Creatress Blessing   61

Part IV
THE JOURNEY OF BECOMING

16. Becoming   65

17. Creativity   67

18. The River of Life   69

19. The River Speaks   71

Part V
YOUR INNER LIGHT

20. Soul Star   75

Our Greatest Gift   77

21. Angel's Wings   79

On Angel's Wings   81

22. Wisdom Keeper   83

Child of the Universe   85

23. The Creatrix   87

The Sacred Creatrix   89

The Sacredness of Life   91

About the Author   93

Also by Madeline K. Adams   95

Afterword   97

INTRODUCTION

*We are each a soul star, here to
create a world of love and connectedness*

Soul Star ~ Child of the Universe is a collection of quotes
and poems from books in the Source and Soul Series.

Allow yourself to dip into these pages and read the
poems you feel drawn towards. They each carry a
message for you to trust in the dark mystery of the
feminine and hear the subtle messages that resonate
within you, they are soul calling you to follow your heart.

This small book weaves together the threads of themes
from the books in the Source and Soul Series.

Our personal soul creates a bridge between the wisdom
in our hearts and the intelligence of the universe.

PART I
AWAKEN THE CREATRESS

A CREATRESS SPEAKS

A Creatress knows that the timeless essence of her soul connects her to innate intelligence and her sacredness.

When you take on the presence of the Creatress,
you step into your empowered true essence
and claim your authentic self; honouring
the Creatress within.

You begin to dance the sacred dance of soul and
Become the maker of your unique soul story.

∾

Claiming her presence can change your life ~

It takes courage to walk the path of a Creatress.
You learn how to live creatively in every moment
your life unfolds before you with elegance and grace
And you feel guided by the subtle wisdom of your soul.

FEMININE ESSENCE

THE FEMININE and Soul are inextricably entwined. When you honour the essence of your inner feminine you create an intimate relationship with your soul.

To own her essence within you
Is to claim her creative powers
As you become a Creatress
Of your unique soul story

This is the path of a seeker,
A quest for self understanding,
To love yourself as you are and
Embrace the beauty of your soul

The core essence of the feminine is creativity
Her search for meaning becomes a search
for the aliveness of a loving heart

PSYCHE

*As you embrace your soul's wisdom,
you give attention to your heart's song.
And your soul's aliveness emanates as
the presence of your wise and loving self.*

Psyche is the Greek word for Soul and Psychology comes from this word *psyche*. A symbol for Psyche is the butterfly which is also a symbol for the transformational power of alchemy.

Psyche/Soul is something we may consider to be outside of ourselves. However it can be found within us as our personally felt sense of soul.

～

The myth of Psych tells of the transformational process that takes her from the innocence of a princess to the empowerment of a goddess. Lessons along her journey pave the way for her to become a confident, self-reliant and self-reflective young woman.

Her pregnancy is symbolic of the creative outcome of her journey ~ a symbol of the potential birth of the sacred self, the divine child within us all.

She becomes a Creatress who understands the nature of alchemy ~ creating, transforming and nurturing new life into all its creative forms.

PART II
THE INNER JOURNEY

SOLITUDE

When you sit in stillness and learn to listen inwardly, deeply and quietly, to know the truth that lives within your heart and to hear the inner voice of your soul; this creates an intimate connection with yourself and you discover ~

> *"Solitude is the greatest gift I can give myself*
> *To listen inwardly without fear or guilt,*
> *With an open and honest heart and*
> *willingness to uncover the truth*
> *of who I am here to become."*

To be able to gift myself times of solitude, to give myself permission to take time out and just be with myself. This is how I came to remember ancient forgotten parts of who I am and know myself as an ancient cave dweller.

CAVE DWELLER

I have been a cave dweller for many moons,
Unaccustomed to the noon day brightness
There is comfort and safety in my hidden haven,
And I rarely leave this place I now call home

I have grown into the subtle shadows
and deep darkness,
Where I commune with my Hestia crone
I love the quiet and the stillness
Where the voices of my soul dance around me

There is a beauty and a truth in the essence of their song
And I know my Being-ness matters
My silence is not silence
It is full of the voices of my soul singing
Listen and you will know
how rich this quiet world is

SOUL WISDOM

PERSONAL SOUL IS our feminine timeless essence that connects us to the sacred in our everyday lives.

Your Soul is subtle and strong and calls out
for you to find the courage to listen with
an open heart and follow her guidance.

It was only when I became lost that I was able to uncover my true path: the path that lead me home to my soul.

When your heart awakens and an aliveness expands into every part of you like molten lava, you become intuitively guided in the direction of your dreams.

Our soul speaks to us through the intelligence
of our heart with vibrations of love that resonate
within every cell of our body as a natural
expression of our inner truth.

YOU ARE NOT ALONE

We don't have to do it all alone
Be present in the moment,
Trust your inner knowing
And connection to Source

To create a life of soul consciousness begins
by showing kindness towards yourself and this
leads to the healing of your heart and your soul.

Cosmic Intelligence comes to us as simple truths
that seem obvious once we learn to perceive them

By connecting to the guidance of your soul,
you are able to make empowering choices,
create new meaning and experience happiness
arise spontaneously from within.

SOUL'S LOVING GUIDANCE

*" It is your soul that guides you when you feel you
have lost your way or feel unloved and unlovable.
It does so with wisdom that speaks to you through
your heart with loving kindness and grace
awakening you to the music within, that carries
the rhythm of your unique song."*

Your soul knows how to lead you on what may seem
to be a meandering pathway, so that you gather the
experiences you need to create a foundation
for your unique soul story.

The inner voice of your soul will never ask of you
to hurt another, for it is a loving voice that wants
the very best for you and those around you

Your heart is the barometer of your soul's truth.
It takes courage to follow the subtle callings of your soul

- to take one small step and then another.....

BREATHE IS LIFE

WE COME into this world and as we take in our first breath we become alive with the energy of the unique individual we are here to be; and when our time has come to leave this earthly existence we breath out our last breath as we let go of our life.

Focus on breath and feel into this moment
allow space and time for something
to grow out of the setting of a seed,
an intention that may come from an idea,
an image, a feeling, or an inner essence
that is your personal soul wisdom

In this way breath is life
So breathe into your essential truth
Be still and listen; feel into your open heart

THE INNER PATH

THE INNER PATH is a journey into the deepest most hidden part of yourself. A place within, where your truth is felt as the vibrations of your unique essence and your soul presence.

Steps Down the Inner Path
Create space
Sit with silence
Step outside the familiar
Discover your inner truth
Use your imagination carefully
Seek hurt hidden beneath anger
Let your creative inner child play
Small steps create the greatest change
Uncover your gifts, become your inner gold
Nurture yourself, hear the calling of your soul
Heal your heart, heal your relationship to your soul
As a Creatress, manifest your life of abundance and joy

PART III
DEEPLY FEMININE
MYSTERY

I AM A CREATRESS

A Creatress sees into a world of beauty and mystery.
She glimpses numinous moments of feminine grace
and she knows how to nourish her feminine soul.

A Creatress knows herself to be a
deeply feminine woman who is ready
to take off her mask that has kept her
hidden and to step into her light.

She is innocent and wise; fierce and loving;
courageous and kind; playful and passionate;
She has an inner light that sparkles with joyfulness
She dances with a graceful flow and
She knows how to honour her personal truth

CREATRESS

I am strong and I am gentle
I embody the energies of the Black Virgin
The Sacred Earth, the Child and the Mysteries

I can feel into the hidden depths of another
And awaken you to the beauty of your soul
Trust in my all seeing, all knowing wisdom

Relax and open to my feminine creative force
Let me guide, nurture, protect and inspire
The potentiality I sense living within you

Trust the great mother of all creation
She who resides within your heart as soul
Mystery and magic are her gifts to you
Become her loving presence as a CREATRESS

SECRETS OF A CREATRESS

When you expand your perceptions and open
to guidance you uncover the subtle secrets of
the Creatress and learn to live creatively
in flow with your feminine essence.

I trust in the natural world
With its beauty and simplicity
that is intelligence that emanates
out of lightness and darkness

"When you claim the freedom
To be your true self
The child within awakens
The wise woman sings her songs of love
The Creatress dances to her own rhythm
In tune with the voices of her Soul."

MY INNER CHILD

There is something about claiming my inner child that allows me to play with life and experience both joy and wonder at the magic all around me.

This inner child self feeds the creativity of my soul and gives me permission to enjoy the journey of my life.

Love's energy can be contagious, so beware
~ you may infect others with feelings of happiness.

Joy that bubbles up from within and I feel a well of happiness arise within me and feelings of joy wash over me which I cannot easily explain.

I feel a harmony with everything in the world
A sense of purpose and overwhelming joy.

DARKNESS AND MYSTERY

THE DARK FEMININE carries the energy of the primal forces of the great mother. Her power is that of magnetic energy, the great attractor within the earth. She can be likened to the negative charge at the South Pole, this place found opposite the North Pole which carries the positive charge. She is negative only in the sense of magnetic power and mystery.

To know her is to overcome your fear of the unknown,
The darkness and the depths of your emotions.
Know the longing in your heart as the magnetic
Mystery of your soul calling to you

LA VIERGE NOIRE

La Vierge Noire ~ the Black Virgin statues of mother and child, can be found hidden in crypts of churches in France. The most famous being La Vierge Noire sous la terre, locked away in the underground crypt at Chartres Cathedral. Some are openly honoured as is The lady of the Pillar also found at Chartres Cathedral, and La Vierge noire at Notre-Dame de la Daurade in Toulouse.

The Black Virgin Statues awaken me to the
dark feminine and her qualities as Virgin
~ meaning she belongs to herself alone,
she is her own mistress with the power
to choose for herself

She does not feel inferior to the masculine,
she is empowered from within herself.
In command of her own voice, she stands in her
own power as equal and other to the masculine

Her wisdom comes from her experiences
of the dark mysteries of life, the natural cycles
of death and rebirth and her intimate
relationship with her soul

∾

Black Virgin statues of mother and child
symbolise the loving, healing power of
the feminine as mother, matter, earth,
and creativity expressed in her child

VIERGE NOIRE

She is small, she is black and she is hidden away
Her eyes seem still yet she gazes directly at me
She can see into the very centre of my being
Reading my truth, the essence of my soul

She psychically embraces me with her love
Blessing me with healing, making me whole
She knows all of me and I no longer feel
that I am invisible or have lost my way

Her presence is magnetic, deep and mysterious
She is alchemy, nature transforming itself
She is Dark Matter ~ Mother of us All

PURE ESSENCE

The Black Virgin represents
the pure essence of the feminine
Like a well-spring of purest water that
arises from a place deep within the earth.

Creativity is her core essential self,
the fountain of her power to manifest
new forms and her connection to Source.

Accept her darkness and own her inner glow,
for they are expressions of your becoming
an awakened soul.

Our relationship with her darkness becomes
the energy source of our healing.

WOMB MAGIC

THE ULTIMATE CREATION source of all humankind is the dark wisdom of the womb that nurtures new life and this darkness is a dimension of potentiality for creativity to begin the magic of manifesting into new forms.

The dark moon phase is the cycle in nature that gives time to nurture new creativity within this dark womb.

There is a black that is negative, a black that is wise and a velvet black that holds the power to heal and transform us.

Alchemy meaning *black earth* is the process of whole making and the essence of her dark creative potentiality.

LOVE TOKEN

Follow your knowing for this changes who you become
Choose wisely and listen for the sound of your own drum

Be courageous, take heart and hear the angels sing
Blessed be and blessed all, as you become a ring
The feminine is a circle that cannot be broken
A symbol of your soul's gift, a love token

There is rhythm and a music that is your song
Learn to hear it call you as you dance along
Being in the flow, with nowhere else to go
Oh what joy, for your true self to show

The brighter your soul's light glows
The lighter your warm heart flows
Loving the beauty that is you
Comes from being real and true
Love begins with you
Share it too

A PERSEPHONE WOMAN

PERSEPHONE'S STORY is a classic tale ~ she journeys into the realms of darkness where she meets the soul dimensions of consciousness and gains knowledge of the sacred mysteries. It speaks of her transformation from innocent maiden to her feminine empowerment as queen of the Underworld

Persephone means ~ *She who shines in the dark*

Become a mature Persephone woman who has an expanded consciousness that is both inner and outer focused. She dips into her inner world of mystery and lives in the outer world of physical form. She is both grounded to the Earth and connected to the Cosmos.

~

Just as some Black Virgin Statues are kept below ground in the crypts of churches, Persephone too lived in the underworld ~ sous la terre ~ in the underworld of soul consciousness.

PERSEPHONE

- She has uncovered her power as a woman who is valued, respected and loved for who she is.
- She owns her sexuality as a natural part of the magnetic powers of her feminine creativity.
- She has become self-possessed, gracious and empowered from within.
- She knows her soul speaks through the whole of her in many subtle ways.
- She has developed empathy and sensitivity and expanded her openness to soul guidance.
- She is grounded in the world of form and at home in the inner world of mystery.
- She shape shifts between the Earth and the Cosmic dimensions of Soul.

LAWS OF THE UNDERWORLD

PERSEPHONE KNOWS the Soul's laws of living and her heart is open to cosmic guidance from Source.

Persephone knows the laws of the underworld,
Where darkness has its own light and real beauty
Can be seen as the core essence within every soul

She is an empowered Goddess comfortable
In her feminine ways of knowing and being
She has glimpsed into the mysteries of all creation

She has learned to listen within and be guided
By the voice of her soul and she has found her way
In this Other World of darkness, instincts and mystery.

Know the soul's laws of living, love all things and let your heart open to the energies of your personal Soul

PERMISSION

She gives herself permission to shine her light
And to withdraw her light into the realms of darkness
To renew herself in honour of the cycles of becoming
Which are the core of her creative essence

Persephone and the Black Madonna are both
archetypal expressions of an ancient primal force
of the great mother. She is mystery unfolding out of
darkness, feminine creative essence and protector to
souls rebirthing or transitioning back to cosmic soul.

She glows in the darkness, becoming a beacon of light
for Souls to follow. Her task is to guide you to reclaim
your Feminine Wisdom and uncover
the hidden gifts of your soul

THE WAYS OF A MODERN MYSTIC

A modern mystic develops her subtle senses
so that she can feel her way in the darkness.
She connects with her body, its instincts and wisdom;
her emotions and her imagination; and she strengthens
her trust in her intuitive and psychic knowing.

∼

Psyche or Soul can be seen and felt as an aura that surrounds us. It is the gestalt of our energy blueprint that energetically expresses the whole of who we are.

Elemental forces and subtle ways of knowing:

Fire ~ Clairvoyance ~ clear seeing
Air ~ Clairaudience ~ clear hearing
Water ~ Clair-Sentience ~ clear sensing
Earth ~ Clair-Cognisance ~ clear knowing

Which is your predominant way of knowing?

MYSTERY AND MAGIC

Persephone has become a modern mystic and she
embraces the intelligence of her soul.

I am mystery unfolding out of darkness,
I am the Black Virgin and the Black Madonna
I personify the powers contained within darkness
I believe in the creative forces of my beloved child
My invisibility is a necessary part of
My mystery and magic

Your relationship with your inner wise soul, guides you to
live a rich life of creative consciousness and your body is
the sacred temple of your soul.

LA VIERGE ENCIENTE

In a small village in France of Cucugnan there is a much travelled golden statue of La Vierge Encienté. She has been taken to Lourdes and then to an art museum in Carcassonne. Then she became lost only to be found abandoned in a locker at a train station in Lille.

She now has her own niche in L'Église de Cucugnan. This is an unusual church with soft pink walls, terracotta doors and crystal chandeliers hanging from the ceiling. Here she remains protected behind a see through screen.

She is considered to be rare. She is only fifty centimetres high and she is dressed in a golden gown. Her foot rests on the head of an angel, and below the angel is a crescent moon and a snake.

She is known as the pregnant virgin, she speaks to me of being pregnant with joyful, creative feminine essence.

A CREATRESS BLESSING

I am an awakened Creatress with
The ability to imagine new possibilities
And create my own unique soul story

I honour the feminine within me
I have the insight of a modern mystic
I know her love is grace unfolding

I am Source made manifest and my soul
powers are the Mystical laws of the Cosmos

PART IV
THE JOURNEY OF
BECOMING

BECOMING

BEING present in the moment with trust in your inner knowing and connection to Source. Practical and magical mysteries combine and you become more than you ever imagined as you step into the world as a Creatress.

Becoming

We are a mystery unfolding in
The dimensions of space and time
With the task to become a unique soul
As expression of Source here on Earth
To listen to our Heart and to know at last
How to embrace Becoming as the Magic of Art

CREATIVITY

CREATIVITY BEGINS in the unseen realms of darkness and evolves out of the experiences of flowing with life. It is the Art of Becoming, embracing a life of unfolding creativity.

The secret to true happiness comes from living authentically and creatively in every moment. As you connect to your feminine essence, you uncover the hidden gifts of your soul.

Life becomes art as we learn to dance
the sacred dance of our soul, in tune with
the core essence of our authentic self
So listen deeply and create an intimate
relationship with your soul; and become
the Soul Star you were born to be

THE RIVER OF LIFE

BEING FULLY present and going with the natural flow of energy, you learn to trust in your inner wisdom as it guides you on your journey to becoming a joyful, loving and creative soul.

Live a Life of Soul
Dance in the river of love
Awaken the beauty in your heart
For it is this truth that heals your soul
A truth that is gracious, loving and kind,
Align your physical presence and soul as one
Embrace the dance of life as magical mystery
Learn to flow as one, living in the river of Love

THE RIVER SPEAKS

This river I sit beside speaks to me of the dance of life
It has a relentless surging power and a flow that
moves constantly onwards as do our lives.
As I watch it's gushing movements,
I find the sounds comforting as though it were
a beloved companion.

Water ripples over stony pebbles and rushes through
the gap between two large boulders.
Waves break around the boulders that disturb its path
making ripples of white and blue and green while
it powerfully surges along below the surface and then
it changes into a serene and gentle flow.

At the riverbank some of the water swirls around rocks
to the left, some moves forward brushing the sides
of the rocks on the other bank, some catches against
boulders and bank to turn and rush in the opposite
direction, before resting in a pool of water behind the
large boulders. Still and going nowhere.

Then at last moving on to join the flow again in a
circular, mini whirlpool motion, rejoining the waters
which open into a widening riverbed.

Further down, the river slows and meanders more gently
making swirling patterns, as it passes the many hidden
boulders in its path.

How like my life this river is. With its times of tension,
drama and passion, its blocks and miss-directions,
its whirlpools, waves and stagnant hollows and then
the gentle meanderings, hardly noticeable when
the water slowly moves again.

This river is clear and true and tells a tale of the
movements that arc the journey of life itself.

PART V
YOUR INNER LIGHT

SOUL STAR

WHEN YOU KNOW YOUR SOUL, your heart begins to heal and this connects you to an expanded awareness of self as a soul star; You are a unique expression of cosmic source here on earth.

We each are a glowing light
A soul star of the night sky
Unique in our aliveness of the
Feminine essence of our sacred soul

When you allow yourself space and time to embrace the truth of who you are, you become a soul star and your presence has the power to change the world with the magnetic forces of your truth and your beauty.

Colour Your World with the Beauty of Your Soul

Your awakened Soul shows itself as a sparkle in the eye and an intensity of light from your aura; illuminating the whole of you with its golden glow.

OUR GREATEST GIFT

We are far more than our achievements,
The quality of our presence is our greatest gift
So become the Unique Soul Star you were born to be

By connecting to the mystery of your soul,
You are able to make empowering choices,
Create new meaning, and experience
Happiness arising spontaneously within you

~

Allowing life's creative processes to unfold
Practical and magical mysteries combine
And you become more than you ever
Imagined your self to be

ANGEL'S WINGS

WHEN YOU LEARN to tap into the mystery and magic of your feminine wise self, you will feel empowered to make new choices and become infused with the passion of the beauty of your soul.

> *The secret to true happiness comes from living*
> *Creatively and authentically in every moment,*
> *Uncover your gifts and share them in the world*
> *With loving kindness and grace.*

> *I allow my soul the freedom to fly into the beyond*
> *as if on angel's wings and return to me again.*

ON ANGEL'S WINGS

I breathe the Universe into me
I pause and hear the beat of my heart
And come to a place of stillness within
I breathe out with gentle flowing grace
Sending my love and caring into the world

I sit within my self and sense my soul
With its gifts of protection and love
I am a soul star in the night sky
A bird that soars and lifts me high
A soul that is both ancient and new

I embrace myself as a modern mystic
As I shape shift between two worlds
An angel wraps her wings around me
Wind caresses me and lets me fly
As if carried on Angel's wings

I know that source is within me,
Feelings of peace show on my face

My heart is open and I glow with grace
My soul speaks my truth for others to feel
Let me walk the inner path so my soul may heal

WISDOM KEEPER

You are the Wisdom Keeper of your Soul

AS OUR CONSCIOUSNESS grows of the subtle energies that
are present in and around us, we know they are the
expression of our unique energy blueprint

The truth of who we are here to become
~ a Soul Star, child of the Universe.

Each Soul Star is surrounded by an aura of authentic
inner light that is the illumined glow of their Soul ~ a
unique expression of Cosmic Source here on earth.

Go deep within and ask yourself ~ *"Who am I?"*
Your soul knows the answer to your question
A Sacred ~ Heart Centred ~ Soul

CHILD OF THE UNIVERSE

You are a child of the Universe
A soul star of the night sky
So love yourself as you are
Sacred Creatress of cosmic love

Become the unique soul star
You were born to be
And shine your inner light
A golden glow for all to see

So listen deeply to hear the
Voice of your soul calling you
Trust in your inner wise soul
And feel it's warmth in your heart

Know the music in your heart
And sing your songs of Love
Learn to dance a sacred dance
And let yourself flow with grace

You are a child of the Universe
A singular expression of soul
A manifestation from Source
And vibrations of 'All That Is'

THE CREATRIX

THE CREATRIX IS PRIMAL POTENTIALITY, a dimension that exists beyond our everyday consciousness. I began to glimpse my connection to her intelligence as the source of my creativity.

The Creatrix is the alchemy of nature transforming itself into manifestations of the feminine face of Source.

The Creatrix speaks through me with beauty and truth. She awakens my creativity and nurtures my soul.

She speaks to my heart with the energy of love. She shows me how to truly love myself and I feel accepted, loved and embraced as I am

Love is the highest vibrational field we can experience as humankind here on earth

THE SACRED CREATRIX

She is small, she is black, she has a beauty all her own
There is truth in her eyes and simplicity in her form
She lives in a world of unseen forces

She understands the mysteries of birth and death
And sees the hidden gold in the heart of every soul
She is the great mother, Creatrix of all life forms

Her greatest works are done in the darkness
She is patient, she knows how to
be still and to sit and wait
For she is incubating her next creation

There is a magic and mystery to her presence
A depth of wisdom and inner knowing
She sees the beauty in all things and loves the
Natural flow of energy we call life.

She hears beyond the words that are spoken to her
She sees into the truth of all matter and
She loves the unique essence of your Being

She is love personified, which heals all things
She embraces you with her wisdom and grace
She is Alchemy, the Presence of the Soulful Feminine
She is the Creatrix of All that Is

THE SACREDNESS OF LIFE

THIS SMALL BOOK is a glimpse into feminine ways of knowing. These words I write came to me out of nowhere; often arriving spontaneously, waking me in the middle of the night. They are words to remind us all of the sacredness of life, the intelligence of Source within us and the presence of our soul.

When you take the journey into your heart you begin a heroine's quest, to create an intimate relationship with your personal soul and to know yourself as a Creatress.

There are liminal moments when we tap into the creative intelligence of the feminine that awakens us to our soul.

The Creatress; the Persephone Woman; the Vierge Noire and the Modern Mystic are all re-awakening Feminine archetypes emerging in todays Aquarian Era.

ABOUT THE AUTHOR

Madeline K. Adams is a Creatress who writes from her heart of feminine intelligence, creativity and soul consciousness. Her vision is to inspire others to walk the inner path that leads them to know the heart wisdom of their soul.

Madeline has taken her inner and outer journeys and she has awakened to the soul presence of the Creatress. She is guided by words from the Creatrix which she describes as '*Words that arrive from the Source intelligence of the Creatrix as she speaks through me in words to touch into my heart.*"

These poems are excerpts from her books ~
The Odyssey of a Creatress
The Sacred Dance of Soul
The Creatrix Awakens (2020)

Madeline is an intuitive Aquarian and Creatress of the Source and Soul Series. She lives in New Zealand

Madeline's Author page
amazon.com/author/madelinekadams

Source and Soul website www.sourceandsoul.com

ALSO BY MADELINE K. ADAMS

Odyssey of a Creatress

~ A Heroines's Journey to Uncover
the Essence of Her Feminine Soul

The Sacred Dance of Soul

~Your Inner Journey to Empowerment

The Creatrix Awakens

~ for publication 2020

Madeline's Amazon Author page

amazon.com/author/madelinekadams

AFTERWORD

One Last Thing.....

If you enjoyed this book or found it useful, I'd be very grateful if you could post a short review. Your support really does make a difference. I read all the reviews personally and I appreciate your feedback.

Thanks again for your support!

Madeline K Adams

To leave a review, use the link below and connect to the review link for this book.

Madeline's Amazon Author page.
amazon.com/author/madelinekadams